Adrift

Michael Allock

Presentation by *BookLeaf Publishing*

Web: www.bookleafpub.com

E-mail: info@bookleafpub.com

ISBN: 9789357442817

First edition 2023

Raindrops

Raindrops languish
west of the autumn sky
as we vanish to the swirling abyss
falling silently forever
on & on
We depart.

A Sparrowhawk's Call

A sparrowhawk on a telephone line
Calls flying
beneath its feet
A dormouse dancing in the rape below
Suddenly becoming prey
Once, hidden. Once, secret.

Now seen.

Does the mother
greeting her long distance son
As she strains to hear his voice
Roughened by adventures new
Know of the bloodshed
to come.

The Vulnerability of Hope

Grey skies will pass
A silver lining must appear
But this truth does not seem to hold
For those who live in fear

Bound and broken
Eroded by shame
Weathered by cruelty
Anchored by blame

A sunrise can startle
As it sheds new light
And shifts the perspective
on what should remain, out of sight

Adrift

An orphan of the storm,
abandoned
Knows nothing but wind
And rain
Pushing defiantly
Fighting an insurmountable tide

Tethered only fleetingly
Lovers entwined
form a fragile anchor
Soon severed, turned loose
With the crashing of the waves

Jagged rocks of broken hearts
provide no respite
From bitter cold, and the sting of the spray
Alone and exposed
Battered driftwood on an open sea
Longing for a stable shore
And a warm embrace,
of sun-baked sand

Escape

A palm swaying in a cool night breeze
Tempers and soothes
An unsettled mind
Distant calls fading away
Tonight there will be no disturbance
Only peace

Stars aligning across an indigo sky
Orion's Belt drifting into view
Pearlescent to heavy lids
A cloud passes on the horizon
Tonight there will be no rain
Only peace

A river trickles across the meadow
The ebb and the flow, welcoming sleep
Downstairs the door creaks open
Heavy boots hit the ground
But tonight there will be no quarrel
Only peace

The Seer's Plea

Cassandra rarely tells of fortune
Of life, and love, away from here
She is but a whisper of madness
Destined to fall on deaf ears

Brighter days foretold
Distant shores call out
The blood of the covenant will save you
Do not give in to doubt

Prophecies of anguish
Of doom and despair
Speaking now of hope
A reputation in need of repair

Before the school run

A hesitation.
He pauses.
The Sun yet to rise
Turning as he steps towards the door

A streetlight's glow
Resting gently on her face
She sighs
Burying her head
Deeper into the embrace of the pillow
Not yet awake
Not yet aware

A final glance
Framed pictures on walls that once surrounded
joy
Now peeling, rotted
No longer supporting,
they strain under the pressure

A suitcase packed in the dead of night
Heavier now
The lock of the door cold to the touch
The warmth of the bed so inviting
But no

A determined breath
And out into the night

A silent tear falls
inevitable, unstoppable
Her head rises
from the now concrete pillow

A hesitation.
She pauses.

The children need composure.

Petrichor in the City

What is that scent they ask
Of fresh grass
and tousled earth
That lingers in the air

The blood of the gods flowing
Through rock and stone
Rejuvenating & refreshing
A parched and stagnant landscape

When they ask
Do you think they long
for such rejuvenation
A hope to refresh their own stale
And stagnant lives

Compare and contrast
A green & pleasant space
With a grey & broken city
Receiving a long-awaited shower

Petrichor in the city? Hardly.
A morning rain
Merely brings the scent
of poverty and hardship

to the fore
A fleeting reminder
sinking into gutters
Past brogues, and past heels
of barely conscious commuters

Haiku 1

A future unclear
Brief reflections on the tide
Lulls bring clarity

Serendipity to the Vine

Serendipity to the vine
Makes an unwitting partner
and fortuitous friend
Of the grand old oak

Sprawling into sunlight
Fuelled by hunger
powered by aspirations
Of canopy life

Innocent surely,
are the vine's intentions
A harmless companion
A brown trunk adorned now with green

Does the vine notice, or care
That yellowing leaves tumble
to the severed branches
and scattered twigs
Blanketing the forest floor
A mighty oak laid bare

Serendipity to the vine.

Untitled Tweet

13

A song once hopeful, now echoes with despair
Eyes once sharp, now succumb to glare
A river once sustaining, now barren & dry
A star once bright, now a lightless, darkened sky

Before the end

Just once more
I'd like to lie
On a bed,
Both lush and green
To feel the warm light
of a glowing midday sun
As soft fingertips,
genially taunt
Thousands of blades
deprived of their ability to cut

Loss, A Universal Experience

15

Scattered galaxies
Of shattered glass
A meteor breaking up on impact
The hand above,
like a crescent moon
Frozen still in the night sky
A nebulous cloud
unable to withstand any longer
The crushing pressure
that comes with the vacuum
created by grief

Haiku 2

Blinking eyes open
Closed hands unfurling wide
A world becomes known

Murmur

Drum-beat rhythm
Filling emptied chambers
A grand manor
Apparently impervious
To the effects of time
Dancers swaying
Draped in crimson
bustling from room to room
Suddenly, they quicken
Steps staccato
A rush for emergency exits
Blocked, hinges broken
Doors sticking
Panic sets
The music
Stops
Dead

Haiku 3

Emerald eyes blaze
Jealousy tending the flame
All devouring

The Myth of Being Out

Even Sisyphus would balk
At the mere thought
Of being out and proud
A Herculean task to tackle
The heteronormative hydra
Open one closet door
And three more pop up in its place
A boulder to be rolled endlessly
A burden never lifted

An ode to Salford

In the city, the streets are alive
With sounds of sirens outside a bar that's a dive
People rushing by, in a never-ending tide
Silence and peace, oh those they couldn't abide

The air is thick, with the long-gone scent of coal
And the smoke of the factories, at its heart and
its soul
The scene of a rat race, with no end in sight
A working man and his everlasting plight

But in this madness, there's still a spark
Of hope and humanity, a fluorescent light in the
dark
The people make Salford, there's no doubt about
that
The matchstalk men, and their dogs and their
cats

www.ingramcontent.com/pod-product-compliance
Lightning Source LLC
LaVergne TN
LVHW050309200726
843509LV00015B/3241